T004027

FRIENDSHIP-BUILDING ACTIVITIES FOR MINECRAFTERS

AN UNOFFICIAL GUIDE

MORE THAN 50 ACTIVITIES TO HELP KIDS CONNECT WITH OTHERS AND BUILD FRIENDSHIPS!

ERIN FALLIGANT

Sky Pony Press
New York

This book is not authorized or sponsored by Microsoft Corp., Mojang AB, Notch Development AB or Scholastic Inc., or any other person or entity owning or controlling rights in the Minecraft name, trademark, or copyrights.

Copyright © 2020 by Hollan Publishing, Inc.

Minecraft® is a registered trademark of Notch Development AB.

The Minecraft game is copyright © Mojang AB.

All rights reserved. No part of this book may be reproduced in any manner without the express written consent of the publisher, except in the case of brief excerpts in critical reviews or articles. All inquiries should be addressed to Sky Pony Press, 307 West 36th Street, 11th Floor, New York, NY 10018.

Sky Pony Press books may be purchased in bulk at special discounts for sales promotion, corporate gifts, fund-raising, or educational purposes. Special editions can also be created to specifications. For details, contact the Special Sales Department, Sky Pony Press, 307 West 36th Street, 11th Floor, New York, NY 10018 or info@skyhorsepublishing.com.

Sky Pony® is a registered trademark of Skyhorse Publishing, Inc.®, a Delaware corporation.

Minecraft® is a registered trademark of Notch Development AB. The Minecraft game is copyright © Mojang AB.

Visit our website at www.skyponypress.com.

10 9 8 7 6 5 4 3 2 1

Library of Congress Cataloging-in-Publication Data is available on file.

Print ISBN: 978-1-5107-6191-9

Cover design by Brian Peterson
Interior design by Noora Cox
Cover and interior illustrations by Amanda Brack

Printed in China

DEAR MINECRAFTER,

Friendship skills are like any other skill. The more you practice making friends and *being* a good friend, the stronger your friendships will get! And the more fun you'll have together too.

This book will give you friendship "boosts" through the Minecraft characters and world you love. Mazes and maps in the **pink-bordered** pages will lead you to new friends. Games and story starters in the blue-bordered pages will help you get to know them better with friendship fun. Puzzles and activities in the **purple-bordered** pages will show you what to do if friendship trouble brews. With every page, you'll feel more confident and grow closer in your friendships.

Ready to begin? Grab your pickaxe—er, pencil—and let's get started!

CONTENTS

The Friends You Have 6

Friendship Paths 7

Map It Out 8

Friends of Many Colors 9

Alike and Different 10

A Good Fit? 11

Offer Up Friendship 12

Study the Situation 13

Spark a Conversation 14

Toss the Ball 15

Tend Your Friendships 16

Would You Rather...? Part 1 17

Challenge Your Memory 18

A Spooky Story 20

Just Joking! 21

Treasure Hunters 22

Friendly Favorites 23

Trade Skills 24

Shared Inventory 25

Make Memories 26

Story Starters 27

Dance Party! 28

Hidden Treasure 29

Five-Minute Fun 30

Prep a Potion 31

Craft a Poem 32

Would You Rather...? Part 2 34

A Pig's Tale 35

Tickle Your Funny Bones 36

Friends and Foes 37

The Enderman's Challenge 38

Play Horse 39

More Story Starters 40

Drawing Duo 41

How Trouble Brews 42

Read the Clues 44

Help a Friend Feel Better 45

Say "Sorry" 46

Before You Blow 47

Switch to Peaceful Mode 48

Choose a Compromise 49

Guard Secrets 50

How Gossip Spreads 51

The Gossip Test 52

Too Competitive? 53

The Good Sport Checklist 54

When Jealousy Strikes 55

When Three's a Crowd 56

Don't Be a Parrot 57

Stand Up for Friends 58

The Good Friend Promise 59

Answer Key 60

THE FRIENDS YOU HAVE

Chances are, you have more friends than you think. Family members can be friends. Teachers can be friends. You may have furry friends and faraway friends too!

Fill in the blanks with your friends' names.

The relative who knows me best is _____.

My favorite pet (real or plush) at home is _____.

I like to video chat with _____.

When I'm having trouble at school, I talk to _____.

At family gatherings, I hang out with _____.

I'd love to live closer to _____.

I have so much fun with _____!

FRIENDSHIP PATHS

New friends may be all around you, waiting at the end of different paths!

In the maze, use three different colors of pen or pencil to find your way to three new friends.

MAP IT OUT

Finding a good friend is like finding buried treasure—sometimes you need to do a little exploring! You might meet friends in your neighborhood, at school, at sports practice, or even in a Minecraft club at the library.

Write down places you might meet a friend in the map below.

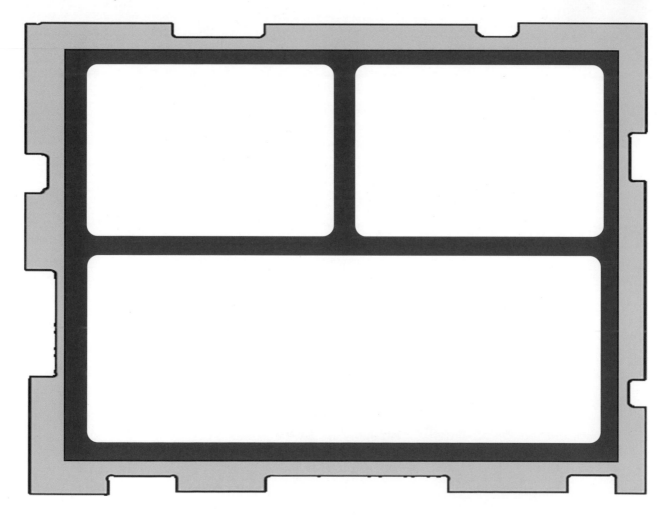

FRIENDS OF MANY COLORS

Clownfish? Angelfish? Red snapper? Just like tropical fish, friends come in all varieties. What do you look for in a friend?

Check off the traits below that matter most to you.

- [ ] Smart
- [ ] Trustworthy
- [ ] Silly
- [ ] Serious
- [ ] Talkative
- [ ] Good listener
- [ ] Brave

- [ ] Adventurous
- [ ] Kind
- [ ] Funny
- [ ] Athletic
- [ ] Creative
- [ ] Loyal
- [ ] Other: _____

Whichever traits you chose, remember this: a friend is someone who helps you feel *good* about yourself when you're around them.

ALIKE AND DIFFERENT

Imagine if your friends were exactly like you. Wouldn't that be boring? Our differences make friendships interesting! Someone who seems different from you might make the perfect friend.

Circle the two creepers who look exactly the same.

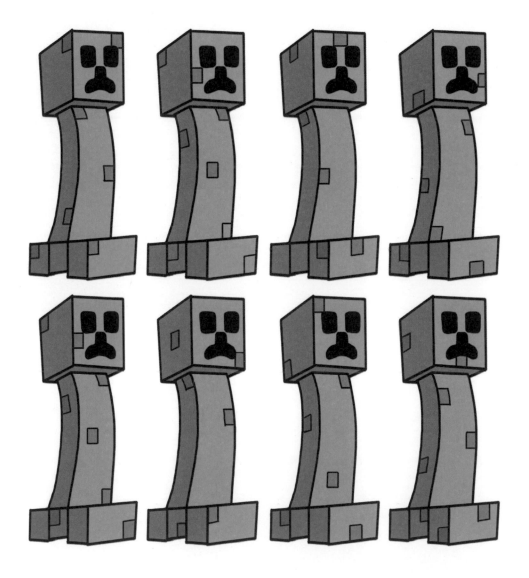

A GOOD FIT?

Friends are like puzzle pieces. Some fit together, and others don't. How can you tell if a new friend might be a good fit for you?

Circle each word that comes right after the word ZOMBIE.

ZOMBIE A CHICKEN ZOMBIE FRIEND RIDE BABY ZOMBIE IS ZOMBIE SOMEONE ELSE ZOMBIE WHO DOES THAT ZOMBIE HELPS ZOMBIE YOU TOO ZOMBIE FEEL LIKE THAT ZOMBIE GOOD ENOUGH ZOMBIE ABOUT TIME STEVE ZOMBIE YOURSELF AND OTHERS ZOMBIE WHEN ARE ZOMBIE YOU'RE THE BEST ZOMBIE TOGETHER.

Write the words you circled here:

_____

_____

_____

OFFER UP FRIENDSHIP

How do you befriend a wolf in Minecraft? You offer it bones until it trusts you. Making human friends takes kindness and patience too!

Check off the things you could offer someone new.

- [ ] Smile.
- [ ] Say hi.
- [ ] Laugh at a joke.
- [ ] Wish someone good luck on a test.
- [ ] Show someone how to do something.
- [ ] Ask to partner up in sports.
- [ ] Invite someone to hang out at recess.
- [ ] Save a seat for someone at lunch.
- [ ] Share your snack.
- [ ] Another idea: _____

STUDY THE SITUATION

Not sure what to say to someone new? Look at what they're doing. Think of one **comment** you can make and one **question** you can ask.

Practice with the characters below.

Comment: *Wow, you have a pet pig. That's so cool!*

Question: *What's its name?*

Comment: _____

Question: _____

Comment: _____

Question: _____

SPARK A CONVERSATION

Asking questions that go beyond yes or no answers can fuel conversations.

Unscramble these words to discover some ideas.

✳ Are you G-Y-A-P-L-N-I _____ a game on your phone? What games do you like?

✳ Hey! What did you do over the K-E-D-E-N-W-E _____?

✳ I like your R-T-H-I-S _____. Where'd you get it?

✳ What did you think of that movie we watched in E-N-I-C-E-S-C _____ class?

✳ I'm V-R-E-S-U-O-N _____ about the game. How do you stay so calm?

✳ What was the D-E-H-R-A-T-S _____ part of the quiz for you?

TOSS THE BALL

A conversation is like a game of catch. One person asks a question. The other person answers and asks another question.

Draw a line between what a friend says and what you might say back.

If a friend says . . .

1. I'm freaking out about the play. Are you nervous too?

2. Hey, do you understand this homework?

3. What are you doing this weekend?

4. Gross. Tuna salad again. What are you eating?

5. I'm working on my dribbling. Can you watch and give me pointers?

You could say this:

A. I have turkey and cheese. Want to share?

B. I'm having a sleepover. Want to ask your parents if you can come?

C. Um, *yeah*. What lines can I help you work on?

D. Sure! Let's take turns.

E. Mostly. Do you want some help?

TEND YOUR FRIENDSHIPS

Nurturing friendships is like growing crops in Minecraft. You have to water and feed them. How do you feed a friendship? With FUN!

Check off the things you'd like to try with a friend.

☐ Invent a secret handshake.

☐ Show off your favorite dance moves.

☐ Name as many Minecraft critters and mobs as you can.

☐ Make up a new game using a basketball or soccer ball.

☐ Come up with nicknames.

☐ Play rock, paper, scissors.
(Or the Minecraft version: block, paper, shears.)

☐ Start a collection of something.

☐ Thumb wrestle.

☐ Build a fort.

☐ Try this tongue twister: *A creeper quickly and quietly crept left and then kept creeping quickly and quietly.*

WOULD YOU RATHER...? PART 1

How do you learn more about a friend? Ask questions—*lots* of questions!

Circle your answers to the Minecraft questions below. Then ask your friend the same questions and circle them with a different colored pen or pencil. If you disagree, talk about why.

Would you rather . . .

❋ Ride a **pig** or ride in a **minecart**?

❋ Be a **witch** or a **spider jockey**?

❋ Live in the **jungle** or in the snowy **taiga**?

❋ Drink a potion of **Leaping** or a potion of **Invisibility**?

❋ Tame a **wolf** or a stray **cat**?

❋ Have a pet **parrot** or a pet **panda**?

❋ Eat a **spider eye** or **rotten flesh**?

❋ Wear a helmet enchanted with **Respiration** or boots enchanted with **Depth Strider**?

CHALLENGE YOUR MEMORY

Being a good friend means paying attention to the little things.

Sit back to back with a friend and answer these questions. Don't peek!

MY TURN

✳ Does my friend have braces? _____

✳ What kind of shoes is he or she wearing? _____

✳ What color is my friend's shirt? _____

✳ Does my friend have freckles? _____

✳ What color are my friend's eyes? _____

✳ Does my friend have glasses on? _____

✳ Is my friend wearing a bracelet or wristband? _____

Now pass the book so that your friend can fill out the next page.

MY FRIEND'S TURN

❄ Does my friend have braces? _____

❄ What kind of shoes is he or she wearing? _____

❄ What color is my friend's shirt? _____

❄ Does my friend have freckles? _____

❄ What color are my friend's eyes? _____

❄ Does my friend have glasses on? _____

❄ Is my friend wearing a bracelet or wristband? _____

All done? Turn around and take a look at each other. How much did you remember?

_____

_____

_____

A SPOOKY STORY

Before reading the story, ask a friend to give you words to fill in the blanks below.

After you've filled in the blanks, read the story out loud. Is it spooky? Silly? Both?

As you and [YOUR FRIEND'S NAME] _____

creep down the tunnel, you hear a growl. "It's a [TYPE OF MOB]

_____!" you cry. "Run!" As you sprint forward,

you trip over a [ITEM IN MINECRAFT] _____. You

smack your [BODY PART] _____ against the ground.

You reach for a Healing potion, but it tastes like [TYPE OF FOOD]

_____. You drank the wrong potion! This one will make

you [ACTION WORD, LIKE RUN] _____ *super* slowly. As

you creep forward, the ground drops out from below. You plunge

downward and land in the [BIOME OR PLACE] _____.

[YOUR FRIEND'S NAME] _____ says, "You made it!"

But when you hear a [SOUND A MOB MAKES] _____,

your heart stops. Something *followed* you . . .

JUST JOKING!

Laughing together keeps friendships going strong!

Ask a friend to help you unscramble the words in the Minecraft jokes below.

❋ How does Steve stay in shape?

He runs around the K-L-C-O-B _____.

❋ What is a creeper's favorite subject?

S-I-S-H _____-tory

❋ How does the Ender Dragon read a book?

He starts at the N-D-E _____.

❋ What did the teacher say to the curious cat?

You sure do O-T-O-L-C-E _____ of questions.

❋ What did the sheep say after it got a haircut?

S-R-A-E-H _____-iously???

TREASURE HUNTERS

When you work together, everything is half the work and twice the fun!

Circle a word and then hand the pen to your friend. Take turns until you've found every "treasure" in this puzzle.

WORD LIST:

ARMOR
BOOKS
CRYSTALS
DIAMONDS
EMERALDS
GOLD
IRON
POTIONS
TNT
TOOLS

V	R	T	S	K	O	A	G	S	N
S	D	L	H	F	Q	R	O	T	G
V	T	O	T	H	D	M	L	J	A
E	N	M	W	O	A	O	D	I	B
Q	T	G	Q	A	O	R	A	T	O
C	R	Y	S	T	A	L	S	C	O
E	M	E	R	A	L	D	S	R	K
X	H	D	I	A	M	O	N	D	S
C	V	J	P	O	T	I	O	N	S
Z	G	B	S	B	I	R	O	N	P

FRIENDLY FAVORITES

Fill in the blanks, writing your answers in the first column and your friend's answers in the second column.

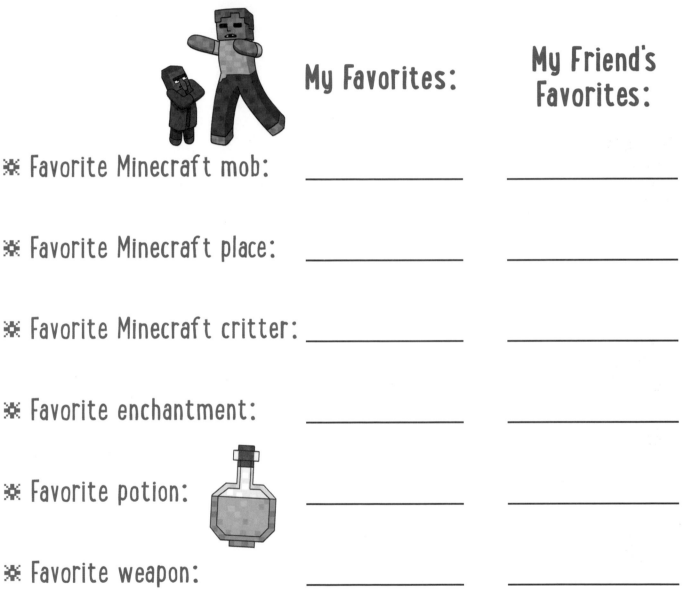

	My Favorites:	My Friend's Favorites:
✳ Favorite Minecraft mob:	_____	_____
✳ Favorite Minecraft place:	_____	_____
✳ Favorite Minecraft critter:	_____	_____
✳ Favorite enchantment:	_____	_____
✳ Favorite potion:	_____	_____
✳ Favorite weapon:	_____	_____

Compare answers. What do you have in common?
Did you learn anything new?

TRADE SKILLS

Like villagers at a market, everyone has skills to trade or teach. Can your friend shoot amazing free throws? Do you know how to whistle on a blade of grass?

Make a plan to swap skills.

I'll teach my friend _____

how to _____.

My friend _____

will teach me how to _____.

Together, we're going to learn how to

_____.

SHARED INVENTORY

Sharing with a friend can be so much fun.

Choose one small thing that you and your friend will share, such as a tiny stuffed creeper. (Ask a parent first!)

We'll share this: _____

Here's who will have it and when:

	MON.	TUE.	WED.	THU.	FRI.	SAT.	SUN.
MORNING							
AFTERNOON							
EVENING							

Here are the rules for taking care of it:

1. _____

2. _____

3. _____

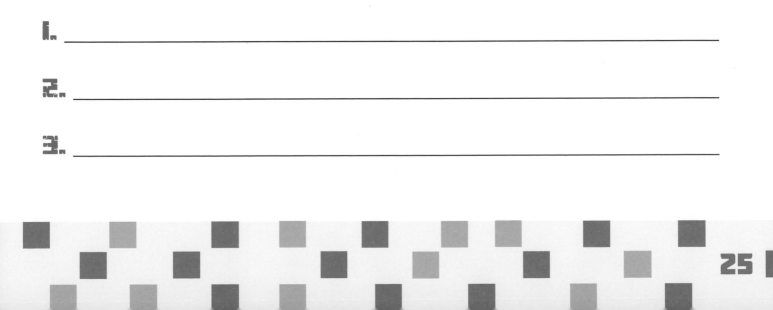

MAKE MEMORIES

Want to remember good times with friends?
Write them down!

Fill in these blanks with a friend or two.

Something we always say: _____

Our three favorite things to do together:

1. _____

2. _____

3. _____

A nickname a friend has for me: _____

My nicknames for my friend or friends: _____

One of our funniest memories: _____

_____

Something we built or made together: _____

Something we'll do together *someday*: _____

_____

STORY STARTERS

Which stories are the most "enchanting"? The ones you and your friends tell together!

Read these story starters out loud, and take turns adding sentences until someone declares "the end."

❋ [Insert Name Here] _____tightened the Elytra wings, took a deep breath, and then raced toward the cliff's edge.

❋ [Insert Name Here] _____ took one last whack with a pickaxe. Something bubbled up from behind the cave wall. Oh, no—hot lava!

❋ As [Insert Name Here] _____ swam through the sunken ship, something appeared in the corner of a waterlogged room. A wooden chest? A *treasure* chest?

DANCE PARTY!

Ask your friends for help putting together the perfect playlist.

Take turns adding songs to the list below. Then turn up the tunes, and dance!

1. _____

2. _____

3. _____

4. _____

5. _____

6. _____

HIDDEN TREASURE

Hide something fun, such as a snack or small gift.

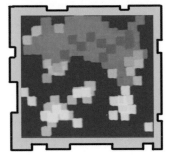

Then fill in this map with clues to help your friends find it. Mark a red X to show where you've hidden the "treasure"!

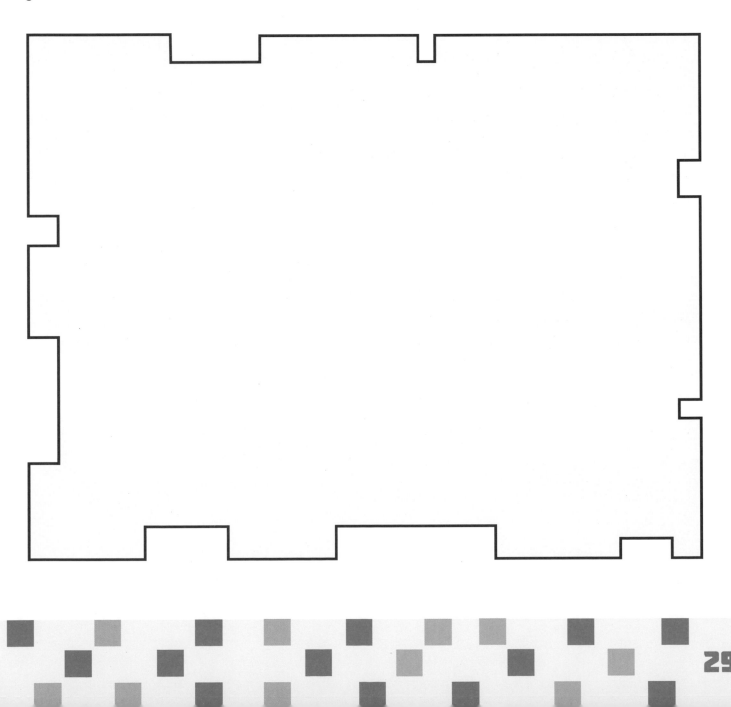

FIVE-MINUTE FUN

Can't decide what to do with a friend? Do it all!

Take turns listing the things you'd both like to do. Then set a timer for five minutes for each activity and check them off your list, one by one.

1. _____

2. _____

3. _____

4. _____

5. _____

6. _____

7. _____

8. _____

9. _____

10. _____

PREP A POTION

Imagine you're brewing potions that no one has ever heard of before. What are they called? What effects do they have?

Brainstorm ideas with your friend. Two brains are better than one!

POTION OF:

_____

POTION OF:

_____

POTION OF:

_____

What it does:

_____

_____

_____

What it does:

_____

_____

_____

What it does:

_____

_____

_____

CRAFT A POEM

Write an acrostic poem for your friend using the first letters of his or her name. Be creative—and kind! Here's an example:

A: Always there for me

L: Likable

E: Excellent Minecraft player!

X: X-tra special friend

Your turn! Write the first letters of your friend's name in the squares below, and come up with positive words starting with those letters.

☐ _____

☐ _____

☐ _____

Now invite your friend to write a poem about YOU.

☐ _____

☐ _____

☐ _____

☐ _____

☐ _____

☐ _____

☐ _____

WOULD YOU RATHER...? PART 2

Circle your answers to the Minecraft questions below. Then ask your friend the same questions and circle them with a different colored pen or pencil. If you disagree, talk about why.

Would you rather . . .

✳ Ride a **horse** or ride a **llama**?

✳ Be an **Enderman** or a **wither skeleton**?

✳ Live in the **desert** or the **extreme hills**?

✳ Drink a potion of **Water Breathing** or a potion of **Night Vision**?

✳ Raise **sheep** or **chickens**?

✳ Have a pet **squid** or a pet **slime**?

✳ Eat a **poisonous potato** or a **pufferfish**?

✳ Use a fishing rod enchanted with **Lure** or with **Luck of the Sea**?

A PIG'S TALE

Before reading this story, ask your friend to give you words to fill in the blanks below. Then read the story out loud.

Time to do chores on the farm! "First, we'll milk the [TYPE OF ANIMAL] _____," you say.

"Next, we'll harvest the [TYPE OF FOOD] _____."

But your friend [YOUR FRIEND'S NAME] _____ keeps eyeing [NAME OF A PET] _____, your pet pig.

"Do NOT try to ride the pig," you say. Too late. Your friend climbs right on. The pig [SOUND THAT ENDS IN -S] _____.

It dodges a [TYPE OF ANIMAL] _____, leaps over a [DESCRIBING WORD, LIKE **FLUFFY**] _____ cat, and crashes into a bunch of [ITEMS, PLURAL] _____.

Your friend flies off and lands in a bucket of smelly [TYPE OF LIQUID] _____. "Are you hurt?" you ask.

"Just my [BODY PART] _____," says your friend with a sigh. "Why didn't you tell me not to ride that pig?"

TICKLE YOUR FUNNY BONES

Keep the jokes rolling!

Ask a friend to help you unscramble the words in the Minecraft jokes below.

* Did you hear about the creeper party?

    It was a L-T-S-B-A _____.

* What do zombies and skeletons wear in the morning?

    Sun K-B-O-L-C _____.

* Why didn't the Enderman cross the road?

    Because he P-E-L-T-O-R-E-D-E-T _____ instead.

* What is a skeleton's favorite instrument?

    The trom-O-B-N-E _____.

* Why aren't there any cars in Minecraft?

    Because the roads are D-K-L-O-E-B-C _____ off!

FRIENDS AND FOES

When friends team up in battle, mobs don't stand a chance!

Circle a word and then hand the pen to your friend. Take turns until you've "battled" every mob in this puzzle.

WORD LIST:

BLAZE
CREEPER
ENDERMAN
GHAST
SKELETON
SLIME
SPIDER
WITCH
WITHER
ZOMBIE

B	Z	W	I	T	H	E	R	H	V
L	W	O	L	U	D	S	R	Z	J
A	A	O	M	D	E	K	E	S	Z
Z	G	U	W	B	B	E	N	P	C
E	H	H	V	P	I	L	D	I	R
T	P	V	A	E	H	E	E	D	E
D	D	T	L	S	Z	T	R	E	E
W	I	T	C	H	T	O	M	R	P
S	L	I	M	E	Q	N	A	C	E
W	V	L	K	L	D	A	N	X	R

THE ENDERMAN'S CHALLENGE

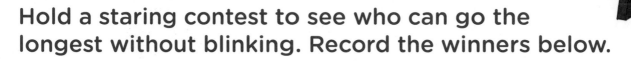

Never look an Enderman in the eye! Unless, of course, that Enderman is your friend.

Hold a staring contest to see who can go the longest without blinking. Record the winners below.

Round 1: Don't blink!

WINNER: _____

Round 2: Eyes wide open!

WINNER: _____

Round 3: Winner of 2 out of 3 takes the Ender pearl!

WINNER: _____

PLAY HORSE

Play "basketball" with a friend or two using a crumpled paper ball and a waste bin.

Take turns shooting. If you miss, write a letter in a box. The first one to spell H-O-R-S-E loses!

Player's name: _____

H	O	R	S	E

Player's name: _____

H	O	R	S	E

Player's name: _____

H	O	R	S	E

MORE STORY STARTERS

Read these story starters out loud, and take turns adding sentences until someone declares "the end."

※ [Insert Name Here] _____ and

[Insert Name Here] _____

struggled against the bubble column, but it was no

use. It sucked them downward toward...

※ [Insert Name Here] _____ uncorked the

potion, tilted the bottle, and took a slow sip. Would the potion

work? It had to!

※ [Insert Name Here] _____ pushed

back a heavy vine. The trees in the jungle were so dense, it

was hard to see. But through a mass of branches, two glowing

eyes peered back . . .

DRAWING DUO

Capture just how fabulous you and your friend are together!

Draw a portrait of you and a friend. Here's the catch: You have to draw your friend, and your friend has to draw you.

HOW TROUBLE BREWS

Imagine you are brewing potions that either heal friendships or harm them.

Which "ingredients" below can harm friendships? Which ones heal them? Circle your answers.

1. Making a friend take your side in a fight

   HARM   HEAL

2. Sharing an embarrassing photo of a friend with others

   HARM   HEAL

3. Taking turns deciding which games you'll play

   HARM   HEAL

4. Telling a friend what they can and can't wear

   HARM   HEAL

5. Telling a friend you're upset by something he or she is doing

HARM   HEAL

6. Bragging about your big win against a friend

HARM   HEAL

7. Letting your friend know you feel jealous

HARM   HEAL

8. Asking a friend why he or she seems mad

HARM   HEAL

9. Getting upset if your friend hangs out with someone else

HARM   HEAL

10. Telling an adult if your friend is being bullied

HARM   HEAL

How'd you do? Make sure to check the answers and tips on page 63, then keep reading for *more* ways to heal friendships rather than harm them.

READ THE CLUES

Can you tell how a friend is feeling just by looking at his or her face? Most people give off clues.

Study each face below, and write what you think each person is feeling.

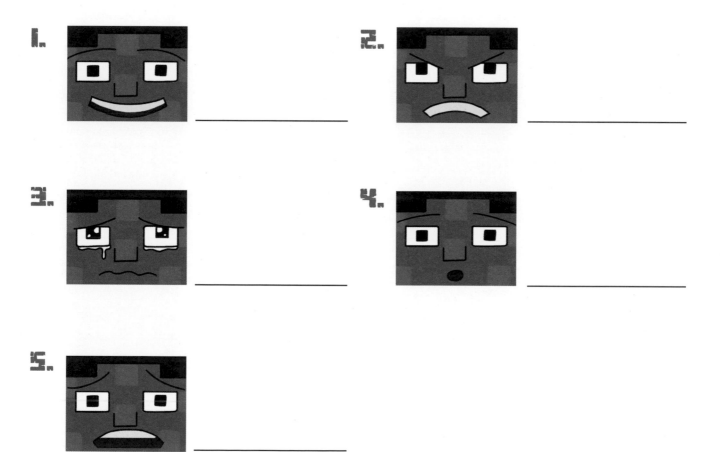

1. _____

2. _____

3. _____

4. _____

5. _____

Not sure if you're right? There's one way to find out: ASK! Asking friends how they feel shows them that you care.

HELP A FRIEND FEEL BETTER

Everyone goes through tough times. Friends can help with the bumps.

Check off the things you could do to help a friend who is upset. Can you think of three more?

☐ Tell a joke.

☐ Give your friend a hug.

☐ Write a nice note.

☐ Share a snack.

☐ Ask if they want to talk.

☐ _____

☐ _____

☐ _____

SAY "SORRY"

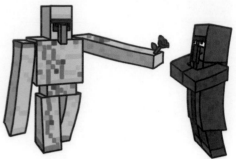

Is a friend upset with you? We all do or say things we shouldn't sometimes. What matters most is that we apologize and try to make things right.

Rearrange these words to spell out an apology.

1. SORRY I'M

_____

2. THAT WON'T DO I AGAIN

_____

_____

3. DIFFERENTLY DO NEXT I'LL THINGS TIME

_____

_____

BEFORE YOU BLOW

Is a friend doing something that bothers you? Say so—*before* you get angry. If you wait until you're mad, you might say things you'll regret!

Follow these steps for saying how you feel:

1. Talk to your friend, NOT to anyone else—and not in front of a bunch of other people.

2. Start with the words "I feel…" instead of "You always (do this or that)…" That way, your friend won't feel like you're pointing your finger and might be more likely to listen.

3. Let your friend know what you want them to do differently.

Ready to practice? Imagine that Steve is upset with Alex because he thinks she's going too fast. What could he say?

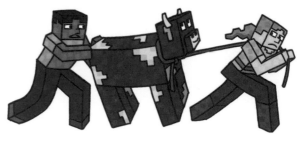

I feel _____ when you go so fast.

I would like you to _____

_____

SWITCH TO PEACEFUL MODE

In Minecraft, battles are optional. The same goes with friends!

To end a fight with a friend, you can choose peace. Which of these ideas could you try?

☐ Make a funny face until your friend laughs.

☐ Agree to disagree. Then change the subject, or switch to a new activity.

☐ Turn things upside down to see things from your friend's point of view. Say, "I see what you're saying. I would probably feel that way too."

☐ Rate your disagreement on a scale of **1** to **10**. If it's a **5 or less**, let it go! If it's a **6 or more**, take time to cool down, and then talk it through.

☐ Find a compromise. Don't know what that means? Keep reading!

CHOOSE A COMPROMISE

Say your friend wants to ride bikes, and you want to go fishing. A *compromise* is agreeing to do something in between, such as biking to the fishing pond. Or setting a timer and doing each thing for a half hour.

Can you find a compromise for each disagreement below?

The disagreement:	A compromise:
Coloring something yellow or pink	
Deciding who will run the last leg of a race	
Baking cookies or a cake	
Building a house with obsidian or cobblestone	

GUARD SECRETS

When friends share secrets with you, they're offering you something precious. They're saying, "I trust you not to share this with other people." So don't! There's only one time when a secret should be shared. When? Solve this puzzle to find out.

Circle each word that comes right after the word GOLD.

GOLD IF YOU WANT GOLD YOU CAN CHOOSE GOLD THINK FOR YOURSELF GOLD YOUR GOLD FRIEND MIGHT GOLD IS ALWAYS GOLD IN A TOUGH GOLD DANGER ZONE GOLD YOU MIGHT GOLD SHOULD ALWAYS GOLD SHARE YOUR TREASURE GOLD THEIR BEST GOLD SECRET HIDEOUT GOLD WITH GOLD AN ADVENTUROUS GOLD ADULT.

Write the words you circled here:

_____

_____

_____

HOW GOSSIP SPREADS

Have you ever talked about a friend behind their back? Be careful! Gossip spreads like a redstone trail. It might quickly spread to someone else, and chances are, your friend will hear it too.

Can you guess where the redstone trail below leads? Follow it to find out!

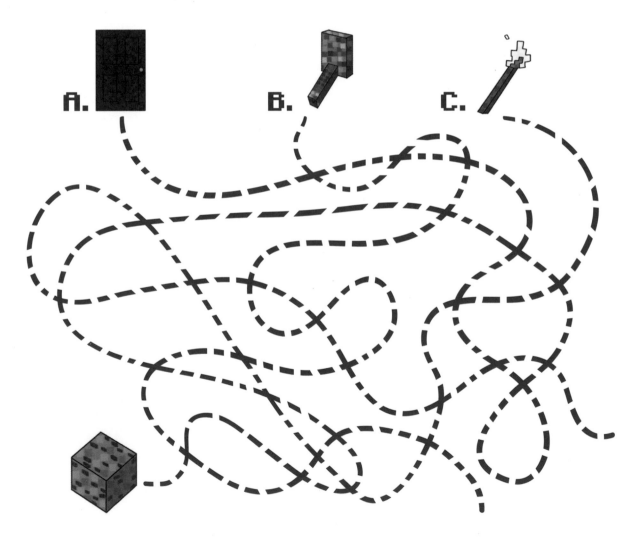

THE GOSSIP TEST

Not sure if what you're saying about a friend is gossip? Take this test.

Unscramble the words below, and then ask yourself these four questions:

1. Would I want my friend Y-G-S-I-A-N _____ this about me?

2. Would my friend feel P-Y-H-P-A _____ if he or she heard that I said this?

3. Could I say this to someone else in T-F-N-R-O _____ of my friend?

4. Is my friend L-E-T-L-G-N-I _____ other people about this?

If the answer to any of these questions is NO, change the subject or walk away. Be careful what you put in a text or email too. Gossip is gossip, whether you speak it or write it!

TOO COMPETITIVE?

Being a good friend means being a good sport, at least *most* of the time. Are you a good sport? Take this quiz to find out.

Check every statement below that sounds like you:

- [ ] My friends say I brag when I win. But what's the point of winning if you can't enjoy the glory?

- [ ] I get mad at referees when they make calls for the other team.

- [ ] When my team loses, it's usually because my teammates didn't play their best.

- [ ] It's *possible* I *might* have cheated a few times in order to win a game.

- [ ] When my friends and I play video games at my house, I go first. (It's my game after all, right?)

- [ ] I usually choose what my friends and I will do, because I have the best ideas.

- [ ] When my friends and I argue about sports, I'm usually right. What can I say? I know a lot about a lot!

If you checked 3 or more, it's time to ask yourself, "What's the point of winning if I end up *losing* friendships?"

THE GOOD SPORT CHECKLIST

Can you unlock the keys to good sportsmanship?

Unscramble the words below to discover what you need to be a *true* winner.

I don't always have to . . .

1. O-S-C-O-H-E _____ what we do

2. Be G-T-R-H-I _____

3. Go F-T-R-I-S _____

4. I-W-N _____

The next time you're tempted to argue, cheat, brag, or boast, remind yourself of these things. Being a good sport takes practice, but it's a goal worth working for!

WHEN JEALOUSY STRIKES

Everyone feels jealous sometimes, but too much jealousy can damage a friendship.

Remind yourself that we all have talents and things that others might envy.

Something my friend has or can do that I envy:

_____

_____

Something I have or can do that my friends might envy:

_____

_____

The next time jealousy strikes, admit it! Say something like, "I wish I could build Minecraft houses as well as you." Your friend will enjoy the compliment, and you'll feel better too! Your friend might even offer to help you.

WHEN THREE'S A CROWD

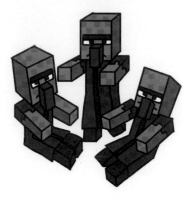

Do you feel left out when a friend includes someone new? Focus on what you can do with three or more people. Can you build a bigger Minecraft house? Battle more mobs?

There's one Minecraft critter that always plays in groups. Connect the dots below to see which one.

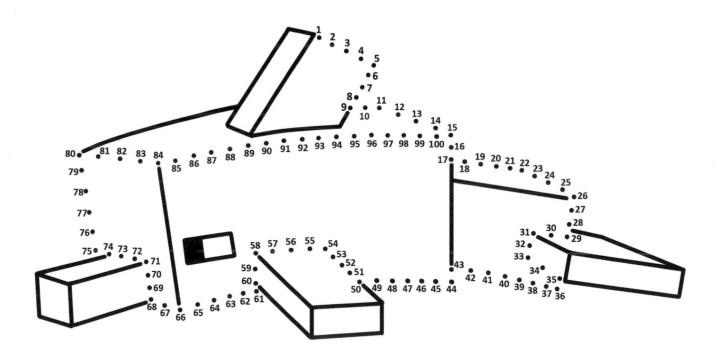

DON'T BE A PARROT

Sometimes it's fun to copy friends—to talk or dress the same way. But there are certain times when you *shouldn't* copy friends.

Do you know when to say no? Check off those times below.

- [ ] When a friend is breaking the rules.

- [ ] When a friend wants to cheat on homework or a quiz.

- [ ] When a friend is being mean to someone else.

- [ ] When a friend tells a lie.

- [ ] When a friend is doing something dangerous.

- [ ] When a friend is doing ANYTHING that makes you feel uncomfortable.

Did you check every box? If a friend pressures you, just say, "No, I don't think so" or "That's not my thing." And remember: TRUE friends won't make you do anything that isn't right for you.

STAND UP FOR FRIENDS

What makes zombie pigmen good friends? They stick up for one another! If one of them is attacked, ALL of them defend their friend.

Check off the things you could try if *your* friend is being teased or bullied.

☐ Say to the bully, "That's not very funny."

☐ Say, "You're bullying. Stop it."

☐ Ask your friend, "Are you okay?"

☐ Go stand by him or her.

☐ Tell your friend that the bully is WRONG.

☐ Say, "C'mon, let's get out of here."

☐ Ask your friend if they want help talking to an adult.

You don't have to do everything on this list. Just do *something*. It'll show your friend you care. And that friend will be more likely to stand up for you if you need it too!

THE GOOD FRIEND PROMISE

Remember this: to have good friends, you have to BE a good friend.

Can you make the Good Friend Promise?

I promise to . . .

* Pay attention to my friends' feelings.
* Help them feel better when they're down.
* Apologize when I need to.
* Admit when I'm upset so we can talk things through.
* Find compromises when we disagree about what to do.
* Guard my friends' secrets.
* Drop gossip before it spreads.
* Try to be a good sport.
* Be happy when good things happen to my friends (even when I'm jealous).
* Include others sometimes when we hang out. The more, the merrier!
* Say "no" when my friends are doing something I don't agree with.
* Stand up for my friends when they're being teased or bullied.

I promise to treat others the way I want to be treated. I promise to be the best friend I can be!

Signed: _____ Date: _____

ANSWER KEY

Page 7

Page 10

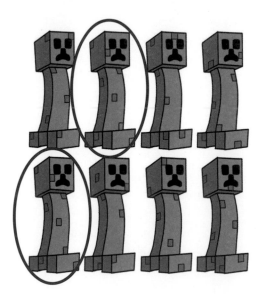

Page 11

A FRIEND IS SOMEONE WHO HELPS YOU FEEL GOOD ABOUT YOURSELF WHEN YOU'RE TOGETHER.

Page 14

• Are you **PLAYING** a game on your phone? What games do you like?

• Hey! What did you do over the **WEEKEND**?

• I like your **SHIRT**. Where'd you get it?

• What did you think of that movie we watched in **SCIENCE** class?

• I'm **NERVOUS** about the game. How do you stay so calm?

• What was the **HARDEST** part of the quiz for you?

Page 15

1. **C**

2. **E**

3. **B**

4. **A**

5. **D**

Page 21

- How does Steve stay in shape?

  o He runs around the **BLOCK**.

- What is a creeper's favorite subject?

  o **HISS**-tory

- How does the Ender Dragon read a book?

  o He starts at the **END**.

- What did the teacher say to the curious cat?

  o You sure do **OCELOT** of questions.

- What did the sheep say after it got a haircut?

  o **SHEAR**-iously???

Page 22

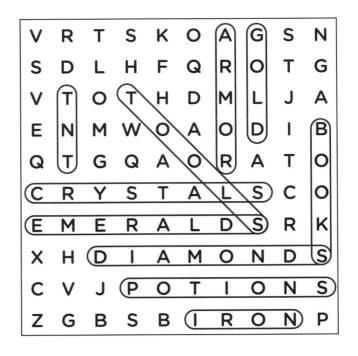

Page 36

- Did you hear about the creeper party?
  - It was a **BLAST**.

- What do zombies and skeletons wear in the morning?
  - Sun **BLOCK**.

- Why didn't the Enderman cross the road?
  - Because he **TELEPORTED** instead.

- What is a skeleton's favorite instrument?
  - The trom-**BONE**.

- Why aren't there any cars in Minecraft?
  - Because the roads are **BLOCKED** off!

Page 37

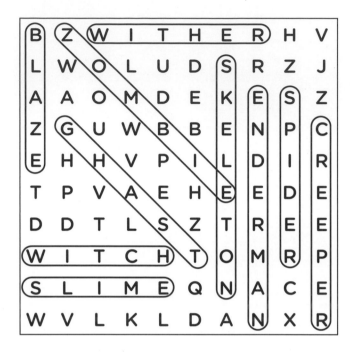

Page 42–43

1. **Harm.** You may *want* your friend to take your side, but you can't demand it. Your friend may want to stay out of the fight, and that's okay!

2. **Harm.** But you knew that, right?

3. **Heal.** Taking turns helps prevent arguments by giving you equal say in what you'll play.

4. **Harm.** Your friends have the right to express their own style, just like you do.

5. **It depends.** If you speak up, you could harm the friendship. But if you express your feelings calmly, you're giving your friend a chance to do things differently.

6. **Harm.** Try to be a good sport, whether you win or lose. Tell your friends what they did well in a game too.

7. **It depends.** Too much jealousy can harm friendships, but admitting it out loud can help you feel better—and it lets your friends know what you admire most about them.

8. **Heal.** You're letting your friend know you're paying attention, and giving him or her a chance to talk things through.

9. **Harm.** Your friends are allowed to hang out with other people, just as you are. Let a friend know if you feel excluded, but only if you're willing to *include* other people when the two of you hang out too.

10. **Heal.** Your friend may not want you to tell, but if you feel your friend is in danger, you're protecting him or her by bringing in an adult.

Page 44

1. **Happy**

2. **Angry**

3. **Sad**

4. **Surprised**

5. **Scared**

Page 46

1. **I'M SORRY**

2. **I WON'T DO THAT AGAIN**

3. **NEXT TIME I'LL DO THINGS DIFFERENTLY** or **I'LL DO THINGS DIFFERENTLY NEXT TIME**

Page 50

IF YOU THINK YOUR FRIEND IS IN DANGER YOU SHOULD SHARE THEIR SECRET WITH AN ADULT.

Page 51

A.

Page 52

1. Would I want my friend **SAYING** this about me?

2. Would my friend feel **HAPPY** if he or she heard that I said this?

3. Could I say this to someone else in **FRONT** of my friend?

4. Is my friend **TELLING** other people about this?

Page 54

I don't always have to . . .

o **CHOOSE** what we do

o Be **RIGHT**

o Go **FIRST**

o **WIN**

Page 56

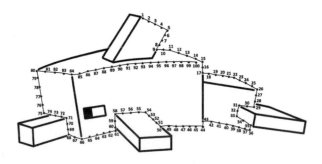